CHILDREN 92 HUTCHERSON 2013
Shaffer, Jody Jensen
Josh Hutcherson

01/28/2013

ACTION MOVIE STARS

JOSH HUTCHERSON

THE HUNGER GAMES' HOT HERO

JODY JENSEN SHAFFER

Lerner Publications Company
MINNEAPOLIS

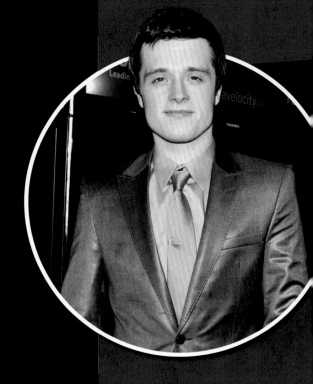

For Tom, Madeline, and Sam.
I love you.

Lerner Publications Company
A division of Lerner Publishing Group, Inc.
241 First Avenue North
Minneapolis, MN 55401 U.S.A.

Website address: www.lernerbooks.com

Library of Congress Cataloging-in-Publication Data

Shaffer, Jody Jensen.
    Josh Hutcherson : the Hunger Games' hot hero / by Jody
Jensen Shaffer.
        p.   cm. — (Pop culture bios: action movie stars)
    Includes index.
    ISBN 978–1–4677–0744–2 (lib. bdg. : alk. paper)
    1. Hutcherson, Josh—Juvenile literature. 2. Actors—United
States—Biography—Juvenile literature. I. Title.
PN3018.H88S53 2013
792.02'8092—dc23 [B]   2012017526

Manufactured in the United States of America
1 – PC – 12/31/12

INTRODUCTION

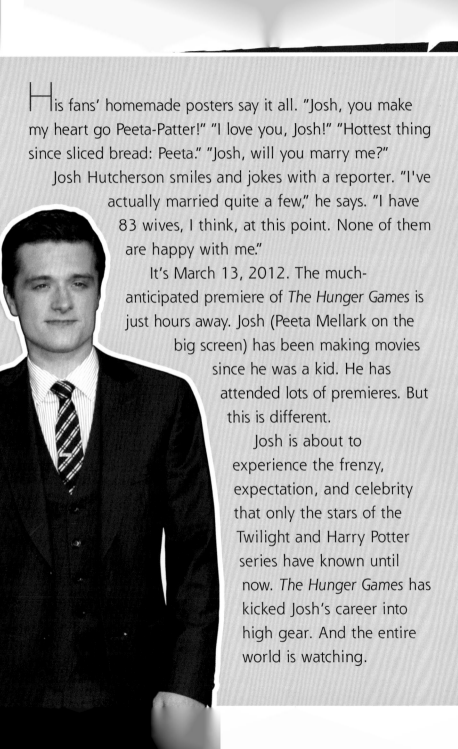

His fans' homemade posters say it all. "Josh, you make my heart go Peeta-Patter!" "I love you, Josh!" "Hottest thing since sliced bread: Peeta." "Josh, will you marry me?"

Josh Hutcherson smiles and jokes with a reporter. "I've actually married quite a few," he says. "I have 83 wives, I think, at this point. None of them are happy with me."

It's March 13, 2012. The much-anticipated premiere of *The Hunger Games* is just hours away. Josh (Peeta Mellark on the big screen) has been making movies since he was a kid. He has attended lots of premieres. But this is different.

Josh is about to experience the frenzy, expectation, and celebrity that only the stars of the Twilight and Harry Potter series have known until now. *The Hunger Games* has kicked Josh's career into high gear. And the entire world is watching.

CHAPTER ONE

CHILD STAR

Josh attends a 2005 movie premiere with his dad, Chris; mom, Michelle; and younger brother, Connor.

Josh in 2003

Joshua Ryan Hutcherson was born in Union, Kentucky, on October 12, 1992. His mother, Michelle, was an emergency response trainer for Delta Airlines. She later quit her job to help support Josh's acting career. Josh's dad, Chris, works for the government. Josh has a younger brother, Connor, and Josh grew up with tons of pets.

As early as the age of three, Josh loved being the center of attention. He'd watch TV and think about how cool it would be to be like the actors. Josh begged his parents to let him be in movies. They wanted him to try sports instead.

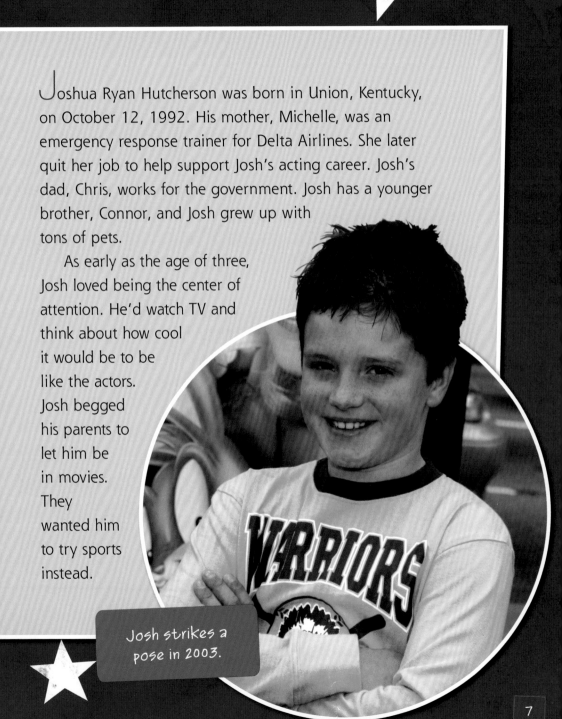

Josh strikes a pose in 2003.

When Josh turned nine, his parents said he could look into acting. Josh grabbed the Yellow Pages and found Bob Luke, an acting coach. Bob was impressed with Josh. He told Josh to go to Los Angeles, get an agent, and try out for movie and TV roles.

But Josh's parents were still unsure. Josh had never acted in anything besides a TV ad and a Vacation Bible School film. Finally, they said Josh could go. They gave him one pilot season to see if he could find work. Josh and his mom packed their bags. They rented an apartment in Studio City, California.

AGENT = a person who finds jobs for actors

PILOT SEASON = the brief time period each year when TV stations test new shows in front of audiences

Josh's mom, Michelle, moved out to California with him in 2002. This photo is from 2012.

Boy Next Door

Josh quickly got an agent and started auditioning. He was perfect for boy-next-door roles. Josh landed a lead in the TV movie *House Blend*. His career took off. It was 2002. Josh was ten years old.

Over the next two years, Josh did TV episodes of *ER*, *The Division*, and *Line of Fire*. He played in TV movies, including *Miracle Dogs* and *Wilder Days*. Josh was nominated for a Young Artist Award for Leading Young Actor for *Wilder Days*. He didn't win. But he was still super excited that he'd been recognized for his role as an eleven-year-old who goes on a cross-country adventure with his grandpa. Josh also appeared in the feature film *American Splendor*.

Josh in 2004

Josh was even busier in 2004. He did voice-over work for the animated TV show *Justice League*. He played TJ in the movie *Motocross Kids*. Josh was Eddie in the TV movie *Eddie's Father*. He did motion-capture work as one of the Hero Boys in *The Polar Express*. And he voiced the character Markl in the English version of *Howl's Moving Castle*. Whew!

Daily Juggle

Juggling an acting career in Hollywood and a normal life in Kentucky wasn't easy. Half the year, Josh was with his mom in Los Angeles or on location for a movie. Josh's dad and Connor were in Kentucky. Josh didn't like being away from his dad, brother, and friends.

School was also tricky. When Josh was not on the set, his mom taught him. Later, Josh had a tutor. Josh's parents tried to keep life as normal as they could for Josh. Even though he was making money, they didn't let him buy whatever he wanted. And he still had to do chores.

Josh goofs around with his brother, Connor, at a premiere in 2005. Josh missed his brother while living in L.A.

JOSH + CARS = <3

When Josh was a kid, he had a collection of mini remote-controlled race cars. Someday Josh and his dad plan to restore Josh's dream car, a 1969 Camaro Z28.

High Gear

Josh kept up his wild pace through 2005. He acted in *Kicking & Screaming* with Will Ferrell. Josh scored a Young Artist Award for his portrayal of Walter in *Zathura*. And he got his very first lead in a movie. He played Gabe in *Little Manhattan*. Another exciting thing about *Little Manhattan*? Josh had his first on-screen kiss in the film. He smooched his costar, Charlie Ray—the lucky girl!

Josh and Will Ferrell attend the *Kicking & Screaming* premiere in 2005.

In 2006, Josh began playing roles that were PG-13. He played Robin Williams's son, Carl, in the movie *RV*. During filming, Josh became supertight with Williams's real thirteen-year-old son, Cody. The boys skateboarded around Vancouver, Canada, where the movie was shot.

Josh became good friends with Cody Williams (RIGHT) while shooting *RV* with Cody's dad, Robin Williams (LEFT). This father-son pic is from 2007.

CHAPTER TWO

CROSSING BRIDGES

Josh and Vanessa Hudgens pose for a pic on the set of *Journey 2* in 2012.

In 2007, Josh got an awesome acting opportunity that blew everything that came before it out of the water. He got to costar with AnnaSophia Robb in *Bridge to Terabithia*. *Bridge to Terabithia* is based on a beloved children's novel. It tells the story of two best friends and the imaginary world they create together. The movie version of the story was getting tons of buzz. It was sure to boost Josh's career to the next level. He'd be playing one of the friends in the story, a preteen named Jess Aarons.

Josh and AnnaSophia Robb appear in a scene in *Bridge to Terabithia*.

Josh adored shooting the film's forest action scenes. The forest creatures were added using CGI after the filming. So he used his imagination a lot. The skill he put into the role paid off big time. Josh won a Young Artist Award for Best Performance in a Feature Film—Leading Young Actor for playing Jess. Soon even more people recognized Josh Hutcherson's name.

CGI =
special effects, art, and graphics added to a film. CGI stands for computer-generated imagery.

Josh and AnnaSophia had to imagine the light in

Josh also played another role in 2007—that of Shane in the movie *Firehouse Dog*. Josh's own dog, Diesel, a two-year-old boxer, kept him company on the set. "Diesel is nuts. He's crazy," laughed Josh. "He loves to go to the dog park, but if you throw a ball, he won't chase the ball. He'll chase whatever dog is chasing the ball."

Josh hams for the camera with one of the canine stars of *Firehouse Dog*.

More Projects!

The following years brought even more work Josh's way. In 2008, he filmed *Journey to the Center of the Earth*. He played Sean, the nephew of Brendan Fraser's character. Based on Jules Verne's novel, the movie was a big hit with teens. Josh also made *Winged Creatures* (later renamed *Fragments*) that year.

Josh moved into horror films in 2009 with the super creepy *Cirque du Freak: The Vampire's Assistant*. And in 2010, he won praise for playing Laser in *The Kids Are All Right*.

Another Journey

In early 2011, Josh began filming *Journey 2: The Mysterious Island*. It was the sequel to *Journey to the Center of the Earth*. This time, Josh was on-screen with Michael Caine, Vanessa Hudgens, and Dwayne Johnson.

ISLAND BUDDIES

Who would Josh want beside him if he were stranded on an island? His little bro, Connor! Awww.

Josh and Connor catch baseball game in 2012.

Josh made a big impression on his fellow actors. He and Vanessa grew to like each other. They even dated for a little bit. And Dwayne was blown away with Josh's acting skills. "I was able to have a partner [in the action sequences]," he said. "[Josh] has great poise."

Josh had to get a scuba diving license to shoot the movie. He went to the Bahamas, where he dove into underwater caves and saw schools of barracuda.

Josh makes great apple pies. His specialty is French apple. Nom nom nom.

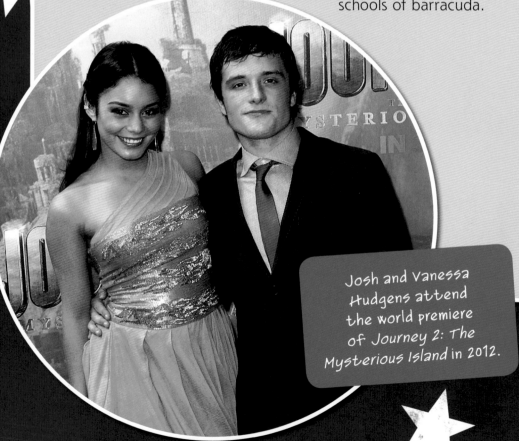

Josh and Vanessa Hudgens attend the world premiere of *Journey 2: The Mysterious Island* in 2012.

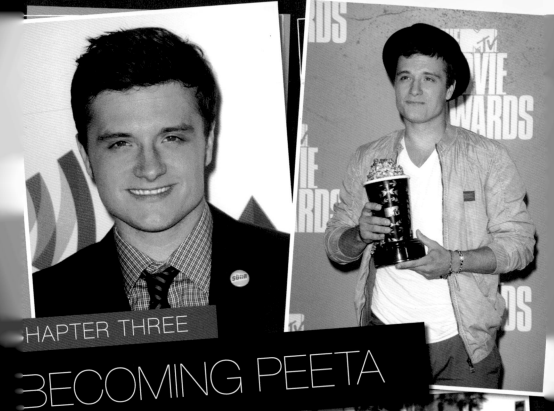

CHAPTER THREE

BECOMING PEETA

Just when it looked as if Josh's career couldn't get any brighter, he learned about plans to make Suzanne Collins's best-selling Hunger Games books into movies. "I read all three Hunger Games books in five days," he enthused. "I couldn't put them down." Acting in the Hunger Games movies would be a dream come true for Josh. When director Gary Ross started auditioning actors for the first film, called *The Hunger Games*, Josh was all over the opportunity!

Josh really wanted to play Peeta Mellark, the baker's son and one of the two male leads. Josh felt he was more like Peeta than any character he had ever played. He liked the way Peeta refused to let anyone or anything change who he was inside. "I've never read a role on the page where I felt that deep of a connection," he spilled.

Josh and Hunger Games auth Suzanne Collins in 20

Josh auditioned in front of both Gary Ross and Suzanne Collins. Talk about pressure! But he must have done well. A week later, he was invited back to do a screen test with Jennifer Lawrence. Jennifer had been cast as the female lead, Katniss Everdeen.

Josh plays basketball three four days a week. He is a hu University of Kentucky fan. H *Hunger Games* costar Jennife Lawrence likes the University Louisville. (Coincidentally, she also from Kentucky.) The two lots of smack when the Unive of Kentucky plays Louisville!

Josh had one final meeting with Gary Ross. Then he waited to hear his fate. The wait was agonizing. "I actually said, 'If I don't get [*Hunger Games*], I don't know what I'm going to do,'" Josh remembered.

Finally, Josh got the call. He was offered the role of Peeta! Together with Jennifer Lawrence and Liam

Director Gary Ross cast Josh as Peeta.

Hemsworth as Gale Hawthorne, Josh would star in one of the biggest movies of all time.

Getting Ready

Josh had about four weeks to prepare for his role. He needed to gain weight and muscle so that he'd look like a fighter. Fighting is a big part of *The Hunger Games*. He ate lots of chicken, and he worked out a ton.

The movie was filmed in the summer of 2011 in the mountains around Asheville, North Carolina. It was really hot. "That was hard," Josh noted. "In the book, they have these special futuristic jackets that keep you cool when it's hot. But with our present technology, it was just hot all the time."

Much of *The Hunger Games* was shot in the mountains around Asheville, North Caroli

Josh said the toughest yet best part of filming was the cave scene with Jennifer. Their characters had gone through a lot by that point in the film. Jennifer's character looks after Josh's character, who has blood poisoning from an injury he got in the Hunger Games. She realizes that she really cares for him and will risk her life to keep him alive. She's willing to leave the safety of the cave where they are hiding to get medicine for Peeta, although Peeta doesn't want her to. The scene was emotional for them both. Josh was pumped about how it turned out. "I've always played sports," he explained, "and that scene kind of had the feeling where your team needs you to nail it. And afterward, you feel like you did."

This scene from *The Hunger Games* shows Katniss and Peeta training for the games.

A Kick in the Head

Josh got hurt while making the action-packed movie. But he wasn't injured in a fighting scene or while making any of the other more dramatic parts of the film. It happened while he was offscreen. Jennifer playfully kicked in the direction of his head. Her foot was closer to him than she thought, though. She gave him a concussion!

Josh and Liam became BFFL on the set, even though they didn't have any scenes together.

Jennifer felt awful about what she'd done. But Josh was fine. He recovered in no time at all. Still, he couldn't help paying her back for kicking him. He put a life-size dummy in the bathroom of Jennifer's trailer to freak her out. It totally worked!

Though Josh and Liam didn't have any scenes together, they became BFFL almost right away. They talked all the time on the set. Instead of siding with "Team Gale" or "Team Peeta," the guys jokingly decided to support "Team Haymitch." Haymitch is Woody Harrelson's character in the movie.

SURVIVOR

Josh thinks his most valuable survival skill is fort making! He made

Jennifer, Josh, and Liam do a Q&A at a mall to promote *The Hunger Games*.

Hollywood Hype

Before *The Hunger Games* premiered, Josh, Jennifer, and Liam toured tons of U.S. malls to promote the movie. Fans waited hours to see the stars in person.

The Hunger Games premiered at Los Angeles's Nokia Theatre on March 13, 2012. Five thousand fans screamed Josh's name as he waved to them. But when *The Hunger Games* was released throughout the country nearly two weeks later, Josh was nowhere near the bright lights of Hollywood. He held a private screening at his home in Kentucky with his family and friends.

Audiences adored *The Hunger Games*. The movie made $155 million in ticket sales its first weekend. It had the third-biggest movie opening ever. After four weeks, the film had made nearly $360 million in the United States alone.

Hunger and Beyond

Josh was involved in several other projects in 2012. These included *Detention*, which Josh starred in and produced; *The Forger*, which Josh also produced and acted in; and *7 Days in Havana*, in which Josh plays the role of Teddy Atkins.

Josh has lots of projects to keep him busy. *Catching Fire*, the sequel to *The Hunger Games*, was filmed in the summer of 2012. It was slated to hit theaters in November 2013. *Journey 3* with Dwayne Johnson is in the works. It has a release date of 2014. And Josh hopes to continue his behind-the-scenes work. He wants to direct and write movies. He and his mom are creating a production company to help Josh achieve his goals.

No matter where Josh's behind-the-screen interests take him, he wants to keep acting. He's been doing it half his life. And according to his scores of fans, he just keeps getting better and better.

JOSH
PICS!

SOURCE NOTES

5   OnTheRedCarpet.com staff, "Josh Hutcherson Talks *The Hunger Games*, Jokes He Has 83 Wives," OTRC, March 13, 2012, http://www.ontheredcarpet.com/Josh-Hutcherson-talks-The -Hunger-Games--jokes-he-has-83-wives-Video/8579305 (June 14, 2012).

13   Rich Copley, "Young Film Star Calls Northern Ky. Home," *Lexington Herald-Leader*, April 1, 2007, http://web.archive.org/web/20070430042435/http://www.kentucky.com/121 /story/31571.html (June 14, 2012).

17   Ibid.

19   Bob Thompson, "Josh Hutcherson Says He Hungered for *The Hunger Games*," Dose.ca, February 7, 2012, http://www.dose.ca/photos/Stroke+awareness+campaign+aims+halve+deat hs/1270270/www.dose.ca/style/Josh+Hutcherson+Says+Hungered+Hunger+Games/6115204 /story.html?id=6115204 (June 14, 2012).

21   Aaron Derr, "Let's Talk," *Boys' Life*, March 2012, 10.

21   Thompson, "Josh Hutcherson Says He Hungered for *The Hunger Games*."

22   Ibid.

23   Chris Hewitt, "*Hunger Games* Stars Talk about the Movie That's Expected to Set Box Offices Everywhere Ch-Chinging," *St. Paul Pioneer Press*, March 16, 2012, http://www.twincities.com/ hewitt/ci_20183908/hunger-games-stars-talk-about-movie-thats-expected?source=pkg (June 14, 2012).

24   Ibid.

MORE JOSH INFO

Collins, Suzanne. *The Hunger Games*. New York: Scholastic Press, 2008. If you haven't already, read the novel that started it all!

IMDb: Josh Hutcherson
http://www.imdb.com/name/nm1242688
Check this site for a listing of Josh's movies and TV credits, a brief biography, and articles about this talented celeb.

Krohn, Katherine. *Jennifer Lawrence: Star of* The Hunger Games. Minneapolis: Lerner Publications Company, 2012. Check out this in-depth biography of Jennifer Lawrence, which also includes info on Josh and Liam.

The Official Fan Site of Josh Hutcherson
http://joshhutcherson.com
Get up-to-date news, photos, and videos of Josh.

Twitter: Josh Hutcherson
https://twitter.com/#!/jhutch1992
Hutch fans will want to read every word the cutie has to say on Twitter!

Williams, Mel. *Stars in the Arena: Meet the Hotties of* The Hunger Games. New York: Simon Pulse, 2012. View photos and get the inside scoop on the stars of the movie.

INDEX

The images in this book are used with the permission of: © George Pimentel/Getty Images, pp. 2, 28 (right); © J. Merritt/Film Magic/Getty Images, pp. 3 (top), 6 (left); © John Shearer/Getty Images for KCA, pp. 3 (bottom), 20 (bottom); © Joe Seer/Shutterstock.com, p. 4 (top); Graham Whitby Boot/Allstar/Sportsphoto Ltd./Newscom, p. 4 (bottom); © Helga Esteb/Shutterstock.com, p. 5; Zuma Press/Newscom, p. 6 (right); © Carlo Allergri/Getty Images, p. 7; © Kevin Winter/Getty Images, p. 8; © SGranitz/WireImage/Getty Images, p. 9; © Warner Bros./Photofest, p. 10; Adam Nemser-PHOTOlink/PHOTOlink/Newscom, p. 11 (top); © iStockphoto.com/Stan Rohrer, p. 11 (bottom); © J.Sciulli/WireImage/Getty Images, p. 12; © Scott Wintrow/Getty Images, p. 13; Michael Germana/Zuma Press/Newscom, p. 14 (top); New Line Cinema/Newscom, p. 14 (bottom); Walt Disney Pictures/Newscom, p. 15; © A.F. Archive/Alamy, p. 16; Adam Nemser PHOTOlink.net/PHOTOlink/Newscom, p. 17; Walden Media/New Line Cinema/Album/Newscom, p. 18 (top); © John Grieshop/Getty Images, p. 18 (bottom); © Graham Denholm/Stringer/Getty Images, p. 19; Everett Collection/Newscom, p. 20 (top left), © Jason Merritt/Getty Images, pp. 20 (top right), 29 (top left); © Eric Charbonneau/WireImage/Getty Images, pp. 21, 25; Moviestore/Rex/Rex USA, p. 22; © Amy White & Al Petteway/National Geographic/Getty Images, p. 23; © LionsGate/The Kobal Collection/Art Resource, NY, p. 24; AP Photo/Katy Winn, p. 26; © Ryan Miller/Getty Images, p. 27; © John Grieshop/Getty Images, p. 28 (top left); © Victor Chavez/WireImage/Getty Images, p. 28 (bottom left); © Bryan Steffy/Getty Images, p. 29 (top middle); © S_bukley/Shutterstock.com, p. 29 (right); © Tiffany Rose/Stringer/Getty Images, p. 29 (bottom).

Front cover: © Lester Cohen/WireImage/Getty Images (main photo); © s_bukley/Shutterstock.com (left). Back cover: © Jason Merritt/Getty Images.

Main body text set in Shannon Std Book 12/18.
Typeface provided by Monotype Typography.